LOL
HUNTING
AND
FISHING

———— • ————

by

Jack Kreismer

RED-LETTER PRESS, INC.
Saddle River, New Jersey

LOL HUNTING AND FISHING
COPYRIGHT ©2013 Red-Letter Press, Inc.
ISBN-13: 978-1-60387-003-0
ISBN: 1-60387-003-2

The Fishing Section contains some items which
have been excerpted from LOL Fishing.

Red-Letter Press, Inc.
P.O. Box 393
Saddle River, NJ 07458

www.Red-LetterPress.com

ACKNOWLEDGMENTS

EDITORIAL:
Jeff Kreismer

•

BOOK DESIGN & TYPOGRAPHY:
Jeff Kreismer

•

COVER
Art by Randa Accessories

•

RESEARCH & DEVELOPMENT:
Sparky Kreismer
Sanford Mims
Kobus Reyneke
Mike "Rifle Arm" Ryan

LOL
HUNTING
AND
FISHING

A hunter thought he came up with an absolutely brilliant idea- to sit in a tree so that other hunters wouldn't mistake him for a deer.

His plan worked. He was mistaken for a bear.

Dan and Dave were trudging through the woods when they encountered the king of the jungle.

"Keep cool," said Dan. "Remember what it says in the book... Stay calm and stand absolutely still while you stare the lion down. Eventually, he'll turn around and walk away."

"That's all well and good," said Dave. "You've read the book, and I've read the book, but has the lion read the book?"

GAME TALK

The perils of duck hunting are great - especially for the duck.

-WALTER CRONKITE

A Grisly Affair

A hunting-lodge operator who shot and killed his common-law wife was brought up on second-degree murder charges in Quebec Superior Court in June 1984. The jury deliberated for close to ten hours before they finally acquitted him. The man had mistakenly taken his wife for a bear.

Daffy Duck had outwitted Elmer Fudd- that vewy, vewy, silly hunter -once again, and decided to celebrate by having a beer with his two of his animal buddies, a deer and a skunk. The bartender served them each a glass of brew and said, "That'll be six dollars."

The deer said, "I don't have a buck."

The skunk said, "I don't have a cent."

Daffy said, "Put it on my bill."

WHAT DOES THE LION SAY TO HIS PALS BEFORE THEY GO OUT HUNTING FOR FOOD?

A hunter goes into a butcher's store and asks for a duck. The butcher says, "We're all out of duck. I've got plenty of chicken, though. How about a chicken?"

"Oh, that's just fine," complains the hunter. "How am I gonna tell my wife that I shot a chicken?"

A Texan on a hunting trip in Australia spots a buffalo in the distance and asks his host, "What's that out there?"

"A buffalo," replies the Australian.

"Buffalo? You call that a buffalo?" scoffs the Texan. "Why we have 'em twice as big back home in Texas."

The Australian host is highly offended by the putdown. A few moments later, they come upon a gathering of kangaroos.

"What are they?" asks the Texan.

"Those are our grasshoppers."

"LET US PREY."

A fellow knocks on the farmer's door. When the farmer answers it, the guy says, "I heard that you have a mule that points out pheasants. That's something I've gotta see to believe."

The farmer welcomed the opportunity to show off his prized ass so he took the fellow out to the field. As they were walking along, the mule suddenly came to a screeching halt and struck a beautiful point. The farmer walked ahead of the mule and up went a big flock of pheasants. This happens over and over- the mule points, and up ahead are the birds. The fellow finally says to the farmer, "I've seen enough. I've got to have that mule!"

The farmer says, "He's not for sale."

The fellow says, "Everything's got a price. Tell me what you want."

The farmer throws out a ridiculous number. "Alright, 50 grand."

The fellow says, "Sold," writes the farmer a check and leaves with the mule.

The next night the farmer gets a complaint call from the mule's new owner. "I went hunting out at the lake today. When the mule saw the water, he went in and all day long he just stood there, belly deep in the pond! What the heck is wrong with this mule!?"

"I guess I shoulda told ya," said the farmer. "He'd rather fish than hunt."

Dead Man Still Goes
Duck Hunting With Pal

Believe it or not, the above headline is an authentic one that comes from an Associated Press story out of Farmington, Illinois. As the tale goes, Dean Goddin may have died but that didn't make him miss a single day of duck hunting with his buddy, Everett Staffeldt.

In keeping with his last request, Goddin's ashes were placed inside a pair of 2-foot mallard duck decoys that Staffeldt, a retired scientist, had originally carved for his own remains!

Then there was the fellow who went to buy some camouflage clothes, but he couldn't find any.

A couple of city slickers decided to give it a go at duck hunting. They bought a retriever, got a license and were good to go.

After spending about a half a day in the blind, the first guy was getting a bit restless. "We spent all this money on the license and the dog and we've got nothing to show for it- not one duck."

The second guy said, "I'm telling you. I think you've got to throw the dog higher."

Horace and Barney are out hunting deer. Horace says, "Wow- look at that, Barney! A gorgeous bald eagle just flew over our heads."

"Oh," said Barney.

Moments later, Horace says, "Hey Barn, did you see that?"

"See what?" Barney asks.

"What are you, blind? There was a big, black bear that just walked behind those rocks over there."

"Oh."

A minute later Horace again says, "Did you see that?"

To save any further embarrassment, Barney says, "Why, yes, I did."

Horace says: "Then why did you step in it?"

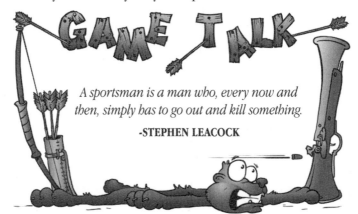

A sportsman is a man who, every now and then, simply has to go out and kill something.

-STEPHEN LEACOCK

Snodgrass was hunting atop the mountains, enjoying the crisp air and scenery all around, when he stepped too close to the edge of the peak and began to tumble down the side of the cliff. In desperation, he grabbed a branch on the side of the cliff and hung there as he looked down 600 feet to the base of the canyon. If he let go, he'd surely plummet to his death. Snodgrass yelled, "Help! Help! Somebody please help me!"

No answer. Again he screamed, but to no avail. Finally, hanging from the limb and looking upward, he said, "Is anybody up there?"

A booming voice replied, "Yes, I'm up here."

"Is that you, God?" Snodgrass asked incredulously.

"Yes, it's me."

"Will you help me?"

"Yes, I will help you."

"How?"

"Let go of the branch."

"What? You gotta be kidding me," said Snodgrass, in a panic.

"Let go of the branch. I will catch you."

After a brief moment of silence, Snodgrass said, "Uh...Is there anybody else up there?"

A hunter noticed that his golden retriever was behaving very sluggishly out on the trail so he decided to bring him to the vet to find out the problem. The vet took one look at the dog, held him in his arms and said to the hunter, "I'm sorry. I think I'm going to have to put him down."

The hunter, tears welling up, said, "But, why Doc?"

"Because he's too heavy."

The husband returns home from hunting and his disapproving wife says, "You didn't shoot anything, did you?"

"I'm afraid I did," the hubby replies.

"You better not have brought it home with you!" the wife says.

He retorts, "We're not cannibals are we?"

WHAT DO YOU GET WHEN YOU CROSS A HUNTING DOG WITH A TELEPHONE?

Bert and Gus are out for some small wild game. Unfortunately, the weather conditions are less than ideal. It's damp and dismal, and what's worse, there's a dense fog thicker than pea soup and the two can't see beyond the tip of their rifles. The two of them take turns taking blind aim and fire away.

Gus shoots first and Bert says, "Did you get anything?"

Gus says, "Judging by the feathers, I'd say it's a pheasant."

A shot rings out from Bert's rifle, and he says, "Judging by the fur, I nabbed a fox."

Another shot rings out in the dense fog and Bert says to Gus, "What do you have now?"

Gus says, "Judging by the documents, it's Wally Smith from Wisconsin."

Then there was the hunter who played golf and got a hole-in-one but went crazy trying to figure out how to mount it.

A GOLDEN RECEIVER!

Teddy and the Teddy

As an historical anecdote, this story has bagged a few smiles through the years and definitely "bears" repeating ...

President Theodore Roosevelt was on a trip down south to settle a border dispute between Louisiana and Mississippi when he was invited to join a hunting party. Being a great outdoorsman as well as a savvy politician, he happily accepted. His enthusiasm was short-lived, however, when he was presented with a bear cub roped to a tree as an easy kill. "If I shot that little fellow I couldn't be able to look my boys in the face again," the appalled Roosevelt sputtered.

The incident was depicted in a "Washington Post" cartoon captioned "Roosevelt Draws The Line In Mississippi." The popular cartoon, in turn, inspired Brooklyn stuffed animal makers Morris and Rose Michtom to create a toy bear for the shop window. It proved to be wildly popular and the Michtoms had to expand their operation to meet the demand for 'Teddy's Bear,' so much so that the business eventually grew into the Ideal Toy Corporation.

And so to Teddy Roosevelt, whose humane act not only gave us the stuff of legend but our favorite stuffed animal as well, bully for you!

Then there was the elephant hunter who got a hernia from carrying the decoys.

An 88-year old hunter goes to his doctor for a checkup. The doctor says, "How ya' doin'?"

The geezer says, "I couldn't be better. I got married a few weeks ago and my 25-year old wife is already pregnant with my child."

"What? That's not possible!" exclaims the doctor.

The old hunter is taken aback and questions the doctor, "What would make you say that?"

"Let me explain," says the doctor. "Since you're a hunter, let me tell you this story. There was a deer hunter who got up real early one morning. He was practically sleepwalking and mistakenly took his umbrella instead of his shotgun. Once he was in the woods and followed some tracks, he sees a huge buck. He takes the umbrella, aims and shoots -boom- the deer drops."

"Wait a minute! That's not possible. Someone else must have fired that shot!"

"Exactly... That's why I'm trying to tell you."

Herb: I've got a really strange dog. When I shoot, he lays on the ground, covers his eyes with his paws and laughs hysterically.

Bert: How does he act when you hit something?

Herb: How should I know? I've only had him for four years.

A novice hunter came back to the lodge and proudly said, "I shot an elk!"

"How do you know it was an elk?" asked one of the members.

"By his membership card."

"I'm here for a gun for my husband," says the woman to the shop owner.

"What gauge did he ask you to get?"

"He didn't," says the wife. "The creep doesn't even know I'm going to shoot him."

Herb and Albert are swapping hunting stories. Herb makes a wide circle with his arms in the air while telling Albert, "I killed an elephant that was this big on my African safari."

Albert laughs and says, "Elephants aren't round, you bonehead."

Herb says, "I was only showing you the eye."

One night during hunting season a police officer, looking for possible DUI violations, was staking out a particularly rowdy country bar noted for the inebriated behavior of some of its patrons.

At closing time, he saw a hunter stagger out of the bar, trip on the curb, and then try his keys in a few different cars before he found his vehicle. Meanwhile, several other hunters left the bar and drove away as he sat in the front seat fumbling around with his keys. Finally, he started his engine, backed up and began to pull away. The police officer was right there, waiting for him. He stopped the driver and administered the breathalyzer test. The results showed a reading of 0.00.

The stunned cop demanded to know how that could possibly be. The hunter replied, "Tonight, I'm the designated decoy."

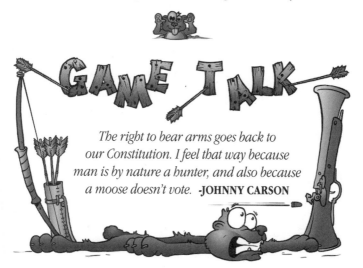

The right to bear arms goes back to our Constitution. I feel that way because man is by nature a hunter, and also because a moose doesn't vote. **-JOHNNY CARSON**

Hal had a yellow Lab named Max. He wanted to show his friend, Herb, the dog's unique hunting ability so they headed down toward the lake. As they approached the water, Hal yelled to his dog, "How many ducks are out there, Max?"

The dog made a beeline for the lake, came back a few minutes later and barked three times. Moments later, three ducks floated by.

"That's amazing," said Herb. "Let me see him do that again."

"No problem," said Hal. Once again he shouted to the dog, "How many ducks are out there, Max?"

The dog took off again, came back and barked twice. Sure enough, shortly afterward, two ducks floated by.

"I gotta show my wife this. She'll never believe it," said Herb. "Can I borrow the dog for a day?"

Hal said, "I don't see why not," so Herb drove off with the dog.

WHAT KIND OF AMMO DO SICK HUNTERS FIRE?

The next day, Herb brought his wife and Max down to the lake so she could witness the dog's amazing ability.

"How many ducks are out there, Max?" said Herb.

Max took off and when he came back, he grabbed a stick, shook it, and then tossed it over his shoulder.

Herb's wife laughed and said, "What's so special about that?"

Herb was flabbergasted and said, "But I'm telling you. He was able to bark and tell me how many ducks were out there yesterday. Lemme try again... Max! How many ducks are out there?"

The dog ran off, came back and did the same thing. He grabbed a stick and shook it, then tossed it over his shoulder again.

Utterly disappointed, Herb drove his wife home and then went back to Hal's place to bring back Max.

"I've got to tell you," Herb said to Hal, "you may be able to get him to count ducks, but I sure couldn't. I said just what you said and all he did was pick up a stick, wave it back and forth and then toss it."

"Of course," laughed Hal. "That's because he was trying to tell you that there were more ducks than you could shake a stick at!"

FLU SHOTS

The Golden Fudd Awards

As a group, hunters are no dumber than anybody else. It is just since they are heavily armed, mistakes tend to get magnified. You can be pretty much guaranteed that hunting season will bring wanton carelessness and bizarre accidents and it is to these unfortunates and their victims that we dedicate the Golden Fudd Awards named for America's favorite incompetent hunter.

A Golden Fudd to...*The duck hunter in Utah who was setting out decoys while his buddy and dog waited in the boat.*

The man had left his shotgun across the bow and the dog was jumping around excitedly, anxious for the day's hunting to begin. It began sooner than expected when the dog jumped on the trigger, blasting the hapless hunter shall we say, below the waterline. The man escaped serious injury suffering only a butt full of buckshot but it does give new meaning to the term "hunting dog."

A Golden Fudd to...*The duck hunters who decided to try their luck on a frozen lake in Michigan.*

They really tried luck's patience when they drove their brand new Jeep out on the icy surface. Naturally if you want to deploy decoys, you need open water so they decided to use a stick of dynamite to blow a hole in the ice. Rather than carefully placing the dynamite and risk a slip while running away, one hunter just lit the fuse and threw it. That's when he remembered that he brought his dog, the dog who liked to play fetch. There wasn't much fuse left on the dynamite when the dog scooped it up and ran back towards his master.

Panicking, one of the men opened fire with birdshot, trying to scare the dog away. He scared the dog all right- right into hiding under the Jeep. All dogs may go to heaven but that Jeep went straight to the bottom. Unfortunately, the hunter learned another bitter lesson when he discovered that insurance companies don't pay off when illegal use of explosives is involved in your claim.

A Golden Fudd to...*The man who decided to "bag" some snakes on south Florida's Alligator Alley.*

Since the road is a main thoroughfare for the slithering reptiles as well as humans, the hunting was excellent but the bugs liked to hunt as well and they were out for blood. Fortunately, our herpetological hunter had the foresight to grab the can of "Off" from under the sink and bring it along. When he was attacked by hordes of mosquitoes, he called for his friend to toss him the can. He sprayed one thigh and then the other. It repelled the insects all right but then transformed his legs and pants into a foaming cauldron of pure agony.

Out of his mind with pain, instinctively, he ran to the nearest water, and disregarding the fact that the place was named "Alligator Alley," jumped in up to his waist. A few minutes later he trudged ashore minus a good deal of skin. His friend was laughing uncontrollably as he handed him the can of "Off" he had dropped in his panic. It seems that it was dark under that sink and the hunter hadn't noticed that the word "Off" was preceded by the word "Easy". Who would have known that heavy duty oven cleaner wasn't good for the skin?

Mantle Piece

Baseball legends Mickey Mantle and Billy Martin were avid sportsmen. This apocryphal tale was a favorite of Mantle's when he was on the banquet circuit.

As the story goes, Mantle and Martin went on a hunting trip to Mantle's friend's ranch in Texas. Upon their arrival, Mantle went in to greet his buddy while Martin waited in the car. While inside, The Mick was asked for a favor. His friend had an ancient mule that was ill and going blind. Because the animal had been with him for years, he couldn't bring himself to put it out of its misery. Instead, he appointed Mantle the task.

With Martin outside and unaware of the request, Mantle saw the perfect opportunity to put one over on his Yankee teammate. Pretending to be agitated, Mantle returned to the vehicle, cursing the ranch owner and vowing to get revenge. Martin, of course, wondered what was the matter.

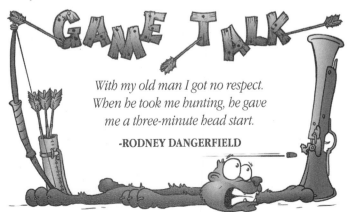

With my old man I got no respect.
When he took me hunting, he gave
me a three-minute head start.

-RODNEY DANGERFIELD

Mantle explained that his "friend" had turned them away and would not let them hunt. "I am so mad at that guy that I'm gonna go out to that barn and shoot one of his mules," he told Martin.

"We can't do that!" Martin exclaimed.

Carrying through with his prank, Mantle pushed Martin aside, stormed into the barn and killed the mule. When he came back out, he saw Martin standing there with a gun, smoke coming from the barrel.

"What did you do, Billy?" said Mantle, a panicked look on his face.

"We'll show that son-of-a-bitch," said Martin. "I just killed two of his cows, too!"

"It seems to me the official (baseball) rule book should be called the funny pages. It obviously doesn't mean anything. The rule book is only good for when you go deer hunting and run out of toilet paper."

-Billy Martin

Upon inspecting the hunter's credentials, the game warden said, "This is last year's license."

"I know," said the hunter. "I'm only shooting at the deer I missed last year."

A young journalist visited a retirement home to interview an elderly but legendary explorer. The reporter asked the old fellow if he could recall the most frightening experience he had ever had.

"Sure can," said the old timer. "A long, long time ago I was hunting Bengal tigers in the jungles of India. I was walking along a very narrow path and my trusty assistant- my gunbearer- was behind me. Suddenly, the biggest tiger I have ever seen leaped right onto the path in front of us. I turned to get my weapon only to find that my assistant had fled. The tiger came toward me with a mighty ROOARRRR! I soiled myself."

The reporter said, "I would imagine, under that circumstance, anyone would have done the same."

The old timer said, "No, no... not then - just now, when I went ROOARRRR!"

As her husband is about to leave to go hunting, his wife says, "If wild game meat is too expensive, you can buy fish instead."

HOW DO YOU TELL IF A MOOSE HAS BEEN IN YOUR FREEZER?

Two guys are out hunting when they come across some tracks in the woods. The first guy says, "Look, moose tracks."

The second one says, "No. Those are deer tracks. I know deer tracks when I see 'em."

A few moments later, they both got run over by a train.

Fred went on safari with his wife and mother-in-law. Late one night, while deep in the jungle, the wife woke up and discovered that her mother was gone. She frantically shook Fred to awaken him. Once he gathered his wits, he grabbed his rifle and the two of them set out to look for her.

At one point, Fred heard some noises up ahead and, as he and the wife came to a clearing, they witnessed a terrifying sight: the mother-in-law was backed up against a gigantic boulder, and a huge lion stood facing her. The wife shrieked, "What are we going to do, Fred?"

"Not a thing," said Fred. "The lion got himself into this mess, let him get himself out of it."

BY THE MOOSE TRACKS

A father took his boy hunting for rabbits. While they were in the woods, they came across some rabbit tracks. In between the tracks were some little brown pellets that caught the boy's eye. He said to his father, "Hey, Dad. What are these little things?"

His father replied, "Those are smart pills."

His son grabbed a couple and immediately spat them out. "These taste awful, Dad."

His father answered, "See, you're getting smarter already."

A hunter making his way through the jungle was surprised to say the least when he saw a pygmy standing next to a dead elephant. Dumbfounded, he said, "Did you kill that animal?"

The pygmy replied, "Yes."

The hunter then asked, "How could a little thing like you kill a giant beast like that?"

The pygmy said, "Simple. I killed it with my club."

The hunter was astonished and said, "My gosh. You must have a gigantic club. How big is it?"

The pygmy answered, "There are 75 of us."

Three duck hunters stood at the Pearly Gates, anxiously waiting to pass through to Heaven. Before they did, St. Peter gave them one strict instruction. "We have lots of ducks here, many of them courtesy of you guys. They're waddling all over the place. There's just one rule here in Heaven. Do not step on the ducks!"

Well, they tried their best, but there were webbed-footed creatures everywhere, and one of the hunters accidentally stepped on one of them.

Along came St. Peter with the homeliest woman imaginable. St. Peter chained them together and said to the hunter, "Your punishment for stepping on a duck is to spend eternity linked together with this homely woman."

A few days later, another of the three hunters accidentally tripped on a duck and St. Peter, who didn't miss a step, locked him in chains for eternity with another extremely homely woman.

The third hunter had seen the fate of his two friends so he stepped very, very carefully everywhere he went. This went on for months until one day St. Peter approached him with the most beautiful woman the hunter had ever seen. St. Peter chained them together, said nothing, and walked away.

The hunter said to the woman, "I wonder what I did to deserve being chained to you forever?"

She answered, "I don't know about you, but I stepped on a duck!"

The season's just begun- opening day and Herb's all prepared. The SUV's loaded up, he's anxiously on his way out the door and suddenly the phone rings. Herb yells to his wife, "If someone asks for me, I'm already gone."

The wife answers, "Yes, he's still here."

"Geez," Herb complains, "I told you to say I left for hunting."

"Yeah, I know, but it wasn't you they asked for."

Clem and Ollie were out hunting when all of the sudden a guy came running out of the bushes, yelling, "Don't shoot! Please, don't shoot! I'm not a deer!"

Clem fired and shot him dead.

Ollie said, "Clem, why did you shoot that fellow? He said he wasn't a deer!"

Clem replied, "Oh! Sorry, I thought he said he *was* a deer!"

Definition of vegetarian: Old Indian word for bad hunter

A bear had an ice cream stand in the woods. One day, a rabbit comes by and asks, "Do you have vanilla ice cream with flies?"

The bear says, "No."

The next day, the rabbit stops at the stand again and asks, "Do you have vanilla ice cream with flies?"

"No," replies the bear again.

After the rabbit leaves, the bear puts on his thinking cap, decides to catch some bugs and whip up some "vanilla ice cream with flies."

Sure enough, the next day the rabbit is back and asks, "Do you have vanilla ice cream with flies?"

"I sure do," says the bear.

"Ewwww...Then give me some chocolate ice cream."

I ask people why they have deer heads on their walls.
They always say because it's such a
beautiful animal. I think my mother is
attractive, but I have photographs of her.
-ELLEN DEGENERES

Terms of En-Deer-Ment

Costing Her Deerly: In Lockport, Illinois, a woman discovered a deer in her basement. Apparently the animal smashed through a window and panicked, taking out the laundry room, plumbing, wiring and other utilities. Animal control showed up, sedated the deer and turned it loose in the woods. No word on who sedated the homeowner who, instead of having a rec room in her basement, now has a wrecked room. Wouldn't it be ironic if she had insurance from the Hartford?

In A Class By Itself: In Port Huron, Michigan, children and parents were at school working late on a PTA project when a deer charged his own reflection in a glass door. They heard the whitetail smashing up the first grade room, tossing chairs, breaking the computer and just generally trashing the place. They couldn't get the deer to stand in the corner but they did manage to shut the door, trapping the deer so that the damage was confined to the one room. One imagines that when the sweet, gray haired first grade school teacher saw what had been done to her classroom, her reaction was somewhat saltier than a simple, "Oh, deer."

WHAT DID THE LION SAY WHEN HE SAW TWO HUNTERS IN A JEEP?

Running For Deer Life: A twelve year old boy in Fon du Lac, Wisconsin, was returning home from the YMCA when he heard a dog bark, turned around and found himself face-to-face with a five foot tall buck who was obviously not pleased to see him. The young man was given a great exercise session as the buck chased him around the parking lot with its huge antlers. He managed to escape unharmed but reportedly won't be watching "Bambi" anytime soon.

The Buck Shops Here: In LaCrosse, Wisconsin, a sporting goods store's grand opening had an ironic twist. Perhaps not being able to bear the suspense of waiting for the customers to come looking for him, a deer crashed through the store's plate glass window to surprise the hunters in their lair. The deer scattered customers and rearranged the stock for a while before someone got the idea to throw a tarp over him. Once disoriented and subdued, one of the more macho customers wrestled the buck by its antlers to eject it from the premises, thus taking away the animal's store charging privileges.

Gomer accidentally shoots Gaylord while they're out deer hunting. He rushes Gaylord to the hospital. After surgery, the doctor says to Gomer, "It was too late. We might have been able to save him if you hadn't taken so much time tying him to the hood of the car."

"MEALS ON WHEELS!"

It was at the crack of dawn and Jethro and Clem had just settled into their duck blind. "I sure wished I'd a brought my TV set with me," said Jethro.

"Why on earth would you want to bring your TV set?" asked Clem.

"Because I left the ammo on top of it."

A sporting fellow is at a social gathering and is boasting to a few people about his hunting expedition. "I was on an African hunting trip and I bagged a few of the biggest tigers you ever saw."

"Hey, wait a minute," interrupted one of the folks. "There are no tigers in Africa!"

The braggart responded, "Right you are, my friend. Not anymore, that is."

A man gets lost while hunting in the woods. Remembering that firing three shots in the air is a signal for distress, he does just that. An hour passes and no one has come to help so he fires three more shots. Another hour goes by and still no help.

Preparing for one more volley of shots, he mutters to himself, "I sure hope somebody shows up this time because these are my last three arrows."

A hunter returning home from a fruitless day in the woods is traveling along a rural area when his car breaks down. He walks along the roadway until he reaches a farmer's house and knocks on the door.

The farmer answers it and says, "I know, I know. Your car broke down. Well, lemme tell you buddy, you can spend the night here, but if you're looking for my beautiful daughter like in the rest of those jokes, you won't find one here."

"Oh, well in that case," says the hunter, "can you tell me how to get to the next farm?"

Ralph and Barney are in a bar in South Africa, about to begin their big-game hunting safari. A friendly chat about who's going to bag the first lion quickly turns into a heated argument. Ralph says, "I'll bet you five hundred big ones, I'll get the first one!"

Barney says, "You're on," and takes a swig of beer. At that, Ralph jumps up from his barstool, grabs his rifle and heads out to the forest.

An hour or so later, a lion walks into the bar and roars, "Anyone in this joint know a guy named Ralph?"

Barney, shaking in his boots, meekly says, "I do."

The lion says, "Well, he owes you five hundred bucks."

Cheney Chuckles

Dick Cheney- you may love him, you may hate him, but you have to admit when the former Vice President's name is brought up in the same sentence as the word "hunting," it's always good for a laugh. Here are some of things the press, the pundits and even the presidents said about that hunting incident back in '06.

"Vice President Dick Cheney accidentally shot a man during a quail hunt, making 78-year-old Harry Whittington the first person shot by a sitting veep since Alexander Hamilton. Hamilton, of course, (was) shot in a duel with Aaron Burr over issues of honor, integrity and political maneuvering. Whittington? Mistaken for a bird." *-Jon Stewart*

"Dick Cheney accidentally shot a fellow hunter, a 78-year-old lawyer. In fact, when people found out he shot a lawyer, his popularity is now at 92 percent." *-Jay Leno*

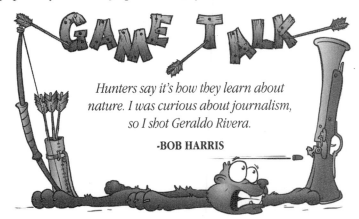

Hunters say it's how they learn about nature. I was curious about journalism, so I shot Geraldo Rivera.

-BOB HARRIS

"He is a lawyer and he got shot in the face. But he's a lawyer, he can use his other face. He'll be all right." -*Craig Ferguson*

"Good news, ladies and gentlemen, we have finally located weapons of mass destruction: It's Dick Cheney."
-*David Letterman*

"The man who was shot is named Harry Whittington. He's a high-powered Republican lawyer. He was very lucky. They say the only reason that he wasn't killed is (because) he was wearing the body armor that never got shipped to our troops." -*Jimmy Kimmel*

"I'll be heading out to do a little fishing with Dick Cheney because the Secret Service won't let me go hunting with him."
-*President George W. Bush*

• President Obama got in on the act during his speech at the White House Correspondents' Association Dinner in 2009, when he said Mr. Cheney was "very busy working on his memoirs, tentatively titled, 'How to Shoot Friends and Interrogate People.'"

• Immediately after the hunting accident occurred, "The Sydney Morning Herald" headlined its story "Cheney Hunts Quail and Everyone Else Ducks."

• "Texas Monthly" won the 2007 Best Cover Line of the Year Award from the Magazine Publishers of America for its January 2007 cover captioned "If You Don't Buy This Magazine, Dick Cheney Will Shoot You in the Face."

A half-century ago, on the hit Russian game show "Bowling for Rubles," two contestants, one from Czechoslovakia and the other from Poland, fought to a draw so both were awarded the first prize, an all expense paid hunting trip to beautiful Siberia.

A few days later, the pair arrived at the hunting camp at the edge of the woods but their guide was sick so they decided to set out on their own in pursuit of the great Russian bear.

After days of tracking a pair of the giant beasts, one male and the other female, they caught up with the bears. The hunters drew a bead on their targets and fired. It was then that they discovered that the "all-expense paid" hunting trip did not include ammo. The clicks of their rifles roused the bears, which gave chase and attacked the hunters.

The Pole was dazed and fell down the riverbank and drifted downstream. Hours later, he came to and made his way back to the camp. He told the guide his story and a rescue party was quickly organized.

WHAT DID THE TURKEY SAY TO THE TURKEY HUNTER?

The searchers trekked through the woods for days without finding anything but then, suddenly, there were the two bears once again. The female bear was still chewing on the hunter's boot when the searchers fired.

The rescuers rushed to the female bear and since it was obvious that they were too late, they grimly set about confirming the fate of the Czechoslovakian hunter. They cut the female open but found nothing and so it dawned on them that this bear's mate must have gotten him.

It was at that point the Pole uttered the immortal words, "The Czech's in the male!"

A guy was visiting his hunting buddy and saw a stuffed lion in his den. "Wow! When did you bag him?," the guy said.

"Two years ago went I went hunting with my wife," was the reply.

"What's he stuffed with?" asked the visitor.

"My wife."

„QUACK! QUACK! QUACK!„

Nate was telling Russ of a great dream he had the night before, one about hunting in the woods- just he and his dog experiencing the beauty of nature and all its trappings. To that, Russ remarked, "Funny, I had a great dream last night, too. I was out on a date with not one, but two gorgeous women!"

Nate said, "Hey, you were out with two women and you didn't think to call me?"

Russ replied, "I did, but your roommate said you went hunting."

Two fellows are hunting in the woods when one of them keels over and falls to the ground. The second guy panics. He calls 911 from his cell phone and says, "Help, help. I'm out here hunting with my friend and he suddenly dropped to the ground. I think he's dead." The 911 operator responds, "Now, now. Calm down. First thing, you have to make sure he's dead."

BANG, BANG!

The hunter says, "Okay, he's dead. Now what do we do?"

And then there were the two hunters who were driving through the woods and came upon a fork in the road where a sign read "BEAR LEFT"- so they went home.

A Rip-Off Inspired By Nature

A lot of guys go hunting hoping to bring home a buck but George de Mestral went hunting and brought home a million bucks- an idea worth a million bucks anyway.

George headed off into the Alps on a hunting trip with his dog in 1941. The pair were soon plagued by burdock burrs sticking to fur and clothing. The unwelcome hitchhikers were so persistent, de Mestral became curious as to how they worked. He took some home and studied them at length. He noticed how the burr's tiny hooks grabbed onto anything with a loop. This gave him a burr-illiant idea.

It took nearly a decade and a half of false starts, rejections, failures, dismissals and ridicule but George eventually found the right methods and materials. His stick-to-it-ive-ness finally paid off with a patent. We know it today as Velcro.

If you think about it, it's odd that a hunter invented Velcro. You'd figure that it would be a fisherman to come up with a product that is the ultimate catch-and-release.

A king was fanatical about hunting and spent virtually all of his time doing so. Finally, the people in his kingdom became fed up with his pastime and overthrew him. In all of history, this is the only known example of reign being cancelled on account of game.

Three men were met by St. Peter at the Pearly Gates. St. Peter said to the first man, "Before I let you into Heaven, I have to know your I.Q."

He replied, "180."

St. Peter said, "Wow- you must have been a rocket scientist!"

"Precisely," the man answered.

"Okay, go on in," said Saint Peter as he turned to the second guy and asked, "What was your I.Q.?"

The guy replied, "160."

"Truly impressive. My guess is that you were a brain surgeon," remarked St. Peter.

"That's right," the second fellow said.

St. Peter welcomed him into eternal bliss, then turned to the third guy. "What was your I.Q.?"

The third guy answered, "73."

St. Peter said, "Not much fun being a game warden, was it?"

Two guys were in the West Virginia wilderness when they came upon an old, abandoned mineshaft. One of the guys threw a rock in to see how deep the pit was, but there was no sound of it striking the bottom. The second guy got a bigger stone and threw it in, but again they heard nothing.

Now they were really curious about just how incredibly deep this mine seemed to be, so they looked for something even bigger to toss down the hole. They came upon a railroad tie and lifted it together, then dragged it over to the pit where they threw it in. As they waited for it to hit bottom, a hound dog suddenly scooted between them and jumped right into the hole!

A few moments later, a hunter approached them and asked if they'd seen a dog anywhere. When one of the guys said that they'd just seen a hound dog leap into the mineshaft in front of them, the hunter responded, "Nah, that couldn't be my dog. He was tied to a railroad tie."

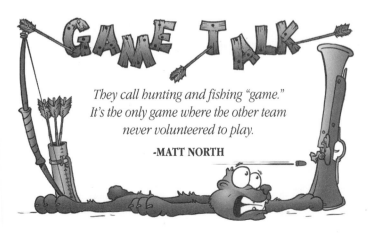

GAME TALK

*They call hunting and fishing "game."
It's the only game where the other team
never volunteered to play.*

-MATT NORTH

A New York lawyer was deer hunting in the backwoods of South Carolina. Making his way through the brush, he was stopped by a grizzled old backwoodsman.

"Hey you! Get out of here! This is private property."

"Listen," the lawyer replied. "You may think I'm a city slicker but I know my way around. This is public property and I can hunt here any time I so choose. I'm one of the top litigators in the country and if you give me any more trouble, I'll sue you and take everything you've got. I'll make so much trouble for you that you'll wish you'd never been born."

"Well city boy, if'n you knew anything at all, you'd know that around here, we don't use courts and judges to settle arguments. We use the Carolina Three Kick rule."

"What's that?" asked the attorney.

The old woodsman replied, "Well, first I kick you three times, then you kick me three times and we go on like that until somebody gives up."

WHAT'S THE DIFFERENCE BETWEEN A HUNTER AND A FISHERMAN?

The lawyer sized up the old man and figured he could take this guy easy.

"OK, you're on," he said, and with that the woodsman landed his thick boot where it would do the most damage. As the lawyer doubled over and slumped to the ground, he wondered how this old guy managed to kick like a mule.

"Here comes number two," the woodsman barked, just as his boot smashed the lawyer in the teeth, knocking him off his knees and scattering his choppers all over the ground.

The woodsman's last kick came with no warning and impacted the lawyer's head so hard it spun him over and over until he came to rest in a briar patch. Severely injured and dazed, the arrogant lawyer struggled to his feet, thirsting for revenge.

"All right, Bubba, you've had your fun," he snarled. "Now it's my turn."

The woodsman shrugged and replied, "Naw- you win. You can hunt here."

A HUNTER LIES IN WAIT.
A FISHERMAN WAITS AND
LIES.

Barney was an avid duck hunter in search for a new bird dog. His search came to an end when he found an amazing dog that could actually walk on water to retrieve a duck. Shocked and thrilled by his find, Barney couldn't wait to show off his wonder dog.

The next day, he went hunting with his buddy, Gilbert, who was never one to get overwhelmingly excited about anything.

"You're not gonna believe what this retriever can do," said Barney.

As they waited by the lakeside, a flock of mallards flew by. They took aim, fired and a duck fell. The dog responded and jumped right into the drink. The dog didn't sink, but instead he walked across the water to retrieve the bird, barely getting his paws wet. This went on all day long; whenever a duck fell, the dog walked on the water to retrieve it.

Gilbert watched the dog do this time and again, but never said a word to its proud owner. Finally, Barney could stand it no longer and blurted out, "Geez, Gilbert. Didn't you notice anything un-usual about my new retriever?"

"Yeah," said Gilbert. "He can't swim."

"I thought you claimed to be the best guide in Maine!" complained one of the hopelessly lost group of hunters.

"I am," said the guide. "But I think we're in Canada now."

A guy comes home from work one day to find his wife dressed in an extremely inviting negligee with a very mischievous look to match. She coos, "Tie me up and do anything you want."

So he tied her up and went hunting.

Two guys were hunting in the forest when all of the sudden a huge grizzly bear appeared before them. They both did an about face and took off running. After a minute or so, one guy came to an abrupt halt, took off his backpack, and pulled out a pair of running shoes.

Meanwhile, when the other guy saw this, he stopped, ran back to the first guy and asked, "Why are you putting on those running shoes? You don't think you're really going to outrun that bear with those, do you?"

The other guy answered, "I don't have to outrun the bear... I only have to outrun you!"

A hillbilly is inconsolable after his hunting dog goes missing. His wife advises him to take out an ad in the newspaper, so he does. But a week goes by and there's still no sign of the missing pooch.

His wife asks, "What did you write in the ad?"

He answers, "'Here boy.'"

Goofy Game Laws

Youse Can't Views Moose From The Spruce Goose

Alaska has a strict law that you are not allowed to even look at a moose while flying. The statute is pretty clear when it comes to airplanes but Rocky and Bullwinkle fall into a gray area.

Water Foul

If you're in the Sunshine State, you had best not be caught hunting a deer while swimming- you swimming that is, not the deer. It seems that Florida feels that hunters who resort to this tactic are all wet.

The Exception To The Rule

In Tennessee, it is unlawful to do any drive-by hunting. The law is very strict- under no circumstances are you allowed to shoot an animal from a moving car. Oh, except whales that is.

Under a law passed by Michigan, there is an allotment of hunting licenses for the blind. This after years of relentless lobbying by the deer.

-NORM MACDONALD

Meanwhile, Back In Alaska...

It seems that some bleeding-heart pro-moose politicians managed to get a law on the books that forbids the time honored tradition of pushing a live moose out of an airplane. Anti-moose forces responded to this onerous restriction on their freedom by passing regulations that make it illegal to serve alcoholic beverages to a moose. In the end though, the anti-moose forces realized their obvious mistake- get the moose liquored up enough and it will throw itself out of an airplane.

Buffalo Bill

While going after big game in Texas, if you happen to shoot a buffalo from the second story of a hotel, settle up your bill because you'll be getting some free state accommodations. Apparently, you can shoot buffalo from the first floor but the second floor, well that's another story.

Violate This Law, Go To Elk-A-Traz

The State Legislature of North Dakota realized that it was something everyone knew instinctively but they felt the need to write it down anyway. It is therefore against the law in the Flickertail State to keep an elk in your backyard sandbox. Apparently some sickos still try to circumvent the law by stashing an elk under their swingsets.

And In A Related Story...

While in Kansas, The Tourism Board asks that you please refrain from shooting rabbits from a motorboat. This has been a public service announcement.

Archie finally decided to tie the knot with his longtime girlfriend. One night, shortly after the honeymoon, he was getting his gear ready for a hunting trip. His wife, standing there watching him, says, "Archie, I've been doing some thinking and now that we're married it might be time for you to quit hunting."

Archie gets this frightfully perturbed look on his face and the wife says, "Archie! What's wrong?"

"You're beginning to sound like my ex-wife," Archie says.

"Ex-wife!" she yells, "I had no idea you were married before!"

Archie answers, "I wasn't."

Bumper Snickers

- *There are no hunting accidents. It's called karma.*
- *We interrupt this marriage to bring you hunting season.*
- *You're In Range- Be Nice To Me*

WHAT'S THE EASIEST WAY FOR A GORILLA HUNTER TO MAKE MONEY?

Putting Lipstick on a Pig

Flagler County, Florida, has beautiful beaches, swaying palms and lots of wild pigs (even when it's not Spring Break). It also is loaded with hunters determined to bring home the bacon.

The story of one such hunter gained widespread notoriety in 2012. He was tracking a wounded pig while his girlfriend was picking wild oranges. Thinking he had his quarry in his sights, he fired. Turns out he had mistaken his girlfriend for the boar and shot her in the leg instead.

Fortunately, the hunter's girlfriend was a cardiac nurse and knew immediately what first aid she needed for her very serious wound.

Unfortunately for the couple, the horror of the accident became a nightmare of national attention.

Jay Leno commented, "I don't know what is worse for the girl: having your boyfriend shoot you in the legs or saying the reason he did it was that he mistook you for a hog. Pretty awful."

The hunter's girlfriend forgave him in a love-conquers-all ending. But, according to the hunter, the embarrassing attention didn't fade until another Florida man committed an atrocity that galvanized the public interest away from him and his girlfriend – the story of the naked man who tried to eat a homeless man's face.

COLLECT UNEMPLOYMENT INSURANCE!

A cop pulls over a hunter driving a convertible because he had a big ol' bear riding shotgun. "Hey, pal, is that a real grizzly?"

"Yeah," said the hunter. "I trapped him in the mountains. I don't shoot 'em. I just catch 'em."

"Well, I suggest you bring him to the zoo."

The hunter agreed, but the next day the cop saw him again driving around with the bear in the passenger seat. "Say, I thought I told you to take that bear to the zoo yesterday," said the cop.

"I did. Today we're gonna see a movie."

A devout hunter lost his Bible while he was out in the woods. A couple of weeks later he's hunting again when a bear taps him on the back. He turns around to see the bear holding his Bible in its mouth. He drops his rifle and takes the book out of the bear's mouth as he looks up at the sky and says, "Glory be! It's a miracle!"

"Not actually," says the bear. "Your name is written right inside the cover."

If a deer hunter says something in the woods and the wife is not around, is he still wrong?

A king was hunting in the forest with several of his henchmen when he spotted a cluster of trees with targets painted in red and white on them. Smack in the middle of each bull's-eye was an arrow. "Who is this incredible archer?" the king wondered aloud. "We must find him."

After many miles of traipsing through the forest, the king and his men came across a small boy with a bow and arrow. The boy admitted that it was he who shot the arrows that were in the center of the targets. The king said, "You didn't just put those arrows into the targets, did you?"

The boy responded, "No, your majesty. I shot them from 100 paces."

"Truly amazing," said the king. "I hereby declare you as one of my royal servants."

The boy bowed and thanked the king for this opportunity.

"Congratulations," said the king. "Just one thing you must tell me as I would like to be able to train more like you. How did you become such a sure shooter?"

"Simple," said the newly appointed young servant. "First I fire an arrow at a tree. Then I paint a target around it."

Harriet's husband Herb, an avid fisherman, died suddenly one day. When she went to take care of the funeral arrangements, the local undertaker asked her how she wanted the obituary to read.

Harriet asked, "What's the cost?"

"A dollar per word," replied the undertaker.

"Okay," Harriet said. "I want it to read 'Herb is Dead'."

The undertaker responded, "I'm sorry. It's a six word minimum."

Harriet thought for a second and then said, "Okay, let's have the obituary say 'Herb is Dead, Boat for Sale'."

Then there was the sad, lonely fish...Seems that after the ocean fishing ship had come and gone he realized that he, in fact, was the sole survivor.

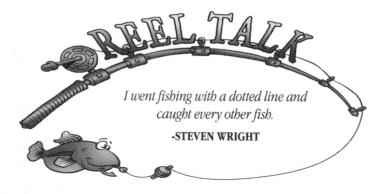

I went fishing with a dotted line and caught every other fish.

-STEVEN WRIGHT

The One That Wouldn't Get Away

A Russian fisherman caught a 28-inch pike and decided to show off his trophy to his buddies. He raised the fish over his head and kissed it on the mouth.

Important safety tip to anglers everywhere: If you are going to kiss a 28-inch pike, make sure that it is dead first. In this case it wasn't, and it clamped down on the fisherman's schnozz. The fish wouldn't let go. The fisherman's screams didn't make it let go. The beating by his companions didn't make it let go. Even the fish's subsequent decapitation didn't make it let go. It took several doctors and nurses in the emergency room to finally pry the fish off. The fisherman still had his trophy, though- a mangled nose mounted in the middle of his face.

Gertrude: You don't really believe your husband's story that he spent the whole day fishing, do you? Why, he didn't catch a single fish.

Gloria: That's why I believe him.

WHAT SWIMS IN THE SEA, CARRIES A WEAPON AND MAKES YOU AN OFFER YOU CAN'T REFUSE?

A guy's terribly sick on an ocean fishing trip. Unaware of this, the captain's mate comes up to him and inquires, "We have complimentary sandwiches on board. Can I bring you one?"

The guy answers, "Naah...just throw it overboard and save me the trouble."

A guy goes on his annual fishing trip to Minnesota. On the boat he notices the seat next to him is empty, so he says to the fellow on the other side, "Wow...to have a no-show on a big trip like this..."

The other guy says, "That's my wife's seat."

"How come she's not here?" asks the first guy. "Is she not feeling well?"

"No. She's dead."

"Gee, I'm sorry to hear that," says the first guy. "But couldn't you find a friend or relative to take her place?"

"I'm afraid not. They're all at her funeral."

THE CODFATHER

Fenwick has a heart attack and dies while on a fishing trip in Montana. The other members of his fishing party are trying to figure out a sensitive way to break the news to his wife. None of them know Mrs. Fenwick, so they elect the local sheriff to inform her since they assume he's had to do that sort of thing before. The sheriff rings the Fenwicks' doorbell. When a woman answers the door, he asks, "Are you the widow Fenwick?"

She responds, "No, I'm Mrs. Fenwick."

The sheriff says, "No, you're not."

A California Fisheries Department inspector boarded the ship that had just come in from a deep sea fishing trip in the Pacific. "I want to inspect your catch," he said to one angler.

"I only caught one fish...this thirteeen pound snapper. Funny thing is, when I opened him up, I noticed he'd gulped down a two pound blue. And inside that blue was this whiting."

"Give me your name and address," commanded the inspector. "That whiting is undersize."

Two parrots are sitting on a perch. One says to the other, "Do you smell fish?"

Wanted Ad

*Woman who can cook, clean, wash and make sweet love.
Must have own boat. If interested, send a photo of the boat
to.....*

When a cop pulls a guy over for speeding, the driver claims,
"Officer, I was just going with the flow of traffic."

The cop says, "Ever go fishing?"

"Yeah."

"Ever catch all the fish?"

There was a sign on a bait and tackle shop which read, "Fishing
Tickle." A customer walked in, told the owner of the spelling
error and then asked, "How long has that sign been like that?"

"Oh, for many years," replied the owner.

"Hasn't anyone else told you of the error?" questioned the man.

"Oh, sure. That's how I get customers."

In the Jersey Pine Barrens, two fishermen were having a high old time sippin' suds and hauling the big ones in one after another. Suddenly, a game warden burst from the bushes and blew his whistle. At once, one of the fishermen dropped his rod and made a break for it. The game warden gave chase as they ran through the briars and brambles. They continued into the pine chiggers along the way. At long last, the fisherman tripped over a stump and fell to the ground, enabling the game warden to catch up.

"Have you got a fishing license, boy?" the warden breathlessly demanded.

"Certainly, sir," replied the angler. "Right here in my wallet," he said, taking out the card.

"Well, you have got to be the dumbest guy I've ever met," said the warden, shaking his head. "Don't you know you don't have to run away from me when you have a license?"

"Yes, sir," said the fisherman. "But you see, my friend back there... he doesn't have a license."

If you can keep your hands in your pockets and make a convincing talk about the fish that got away, you can be a successful salesman.

-MIKE RYAN

A guy walks into a seafood store with a salmon under his arm and says, "Do you sell fish cakes here?"

"No."

"Too bad," the guy says, pointing to the salmon. "It's his birthday."

A small town doctor was a big time fisherman. One day, while on one of his frequent fishing trips, he got a call that a woman at a nearby farm was giving birth. He rushed to her aid and delivered a healthy baby boy. The farmer had nothing to weigh the baby with, so the doctor used his fishing scales. The baby weighed 22 lbs 10 oz.

A fanatical fisherman calls his doctor and says, "Doc, you gotta help me out. It's an emergency. My baby just swallowed a fish hook!"

The doctor says, "Bring him to my office. I'll meet you there."

Before the doctor can even get out the door, the phone rings again and the fisherman says, "Never mind, Doc. I found another fish hook."

Thrashing, Smashing and Trashing

At a shark fishing tournament off Destin, Fl, a captain and three anglers spent over 3 hours battling a 14-foot tiger shark that weighed well in excess of 1,000 pounds.

The first hint that this wasn't going to be an easy catch was that the specially reinforced fighting chair was torn completely off the deck by the furious fish.

Now properly warmed up, the fish proceeded to break two gimbals, a shoulder harness strap, a fighting belt and the spirits of three fishermen who did their best but were exhausted by the battle.

Finally, the well-seasoned captain took over, but the shark managed to swab the deck with him as well before breaking the line and swimming free. The damaged boat limped back to port with the fishermen all empty-handed.

At least the shark will always have the story of the four that got away.

WHAT'S THE DIFFERENCE BETWEEN A GOLFER AND A FISHERMAN?

Harry: How are you supposed to fish on a frozen lake?

Larry: Well, what I do is cut a hole in the ice and then I hold my wrist watch over it. When a fish comes up to see what time it is, that's when I net him.

Smithers had a miserable time of it on the lake, not a single bite all day. On his way home, he stopped at the fish market and ordered catfish.

"Pick out four big ones and throw them at me," he told the fish monger.

"Why would you want me to throw them at you?"

"Because I want to be able to tell my wife that I caught them," replied Smithers.

"In that case, I think you should take the salmon."

"Why's that?"

"Because your wife came in and said that if you stopped by, she'd prefer salmon for dinner tonight."

WHEN A GOLFER LIES, HE DOESN'T HAVE TO
BRING ANYTHING HOME TO PROVE IT.

Murphy was fishing in Maine even though the season was officially closed. A stranger approached him and said, "Have you caught anything?"

"Have I caught anything?" exclaimed Murphy. "I got a couple hundred pounds of the finest rock bass you ever saw iced down in my trunk."

"Do you know who I am?" asked the stranger.

"No."

"I'm the state game warden. Who are you?"

"I'm the biggest liar in the whole state."

The vessel was going down by the bow and the captain of the sinking charter boat came out on deck and asked the fishermen if anyone knew how to pray.

"Yes...I know how to pray," answered a minister.

"Good," the captain said. "Then start praying, Reverend. The rest of us will put on our life jackets...We're one short."

Song Title: *If Today Was a Fish, I'd Throw it Back in*

This Guy's Always Hooking Something on the Golf Course

While searching for a lost ball in a bunker at England's Wetherby Golf Club in 1995, Lennie Learnmouth instead raked in a 40 pound pike.

Heavy rains had caused a nearby river to flood the course, stranding the fish in the bunker until Learnmouth gaffed it with a rake, thus providing him with both the Catch and the Story of the Day at the 19th Hole.

Fishing for Talent

Kevin Constantine, coach of the National Hockey League's San Jose Sharks during the 1990s, made this fishy remark after his squad drafted five players from Finland: "I guess you can say we added some Finns to the Sharks."

HOOK, LINE, & STINKER

Q: What is a frog's favorite sport?

A: Fly fishing

A novice fisherman out on a small boat notices another guy on
another small boat open up his tackle box and take out a mirror.
The novice, out of curiosity, approaches the other guy and asks
why he has a mirror.

"That's for catching the fish. I shine the sunlight on the water,
which makes the fish come up to the top. Then I nab 'em."

"Wow! I'll give you ten bucks for that mirror," offers the novice.

"Done deal."

The novice buys the mirror, then asks the guy, "By the way, have
you caught a lot of fish this week?"

"You're the eighth."

George is lying face down on the road with his ear to the pavement.
A stranger comes up to him and says, "Hey, what are you doing?"

George says, "A green pickup truck, two fishermen in it with their
poles hanging out the back... vanity license plates that say 'Gone
Fishing.'"

The stranger says, "You can tell all that just from putting your ear
to the ground?"

"No. I'm talking about the truck that ran me over a few minutes
ago."

Angus McCorkle, Scotland's most prominent atheist, decided that while most people were wasting their time in church on Christmas morning, it'd be a perfect time for him to go fishing.

He set off in a small boat across Loch Ness until he reached the midway point and dropped his line in the water. All of a sudden, there was a great bubbling in the water. The disturbance grew and grew until McCorkle's tiny boat was lifted high into the air on the great back of the Loch Ness monster, which turned its head, bared its huge teeth and craned its long neck around to reach Angus.

Terrified, Angus cried out, "Oh, God...save me from this terrible beastie!"

From above, a deep voice boomed out, "Angus, I thought you didn't believe in Me."

Angus shouted back, "Come on and work with me a wee bit, Lord. Ten minutes ago, I didn't believe in the Loch Ness monster either!"

If people concentrated on the really important things in life, there'd be a shortage of fishing poles.

-DOUG LARSON

A Whole New Meaning to "Rapping" a Fish

Remember when America declared a psychological war on
Panamanian dictator Manuel Noriega and blared hard rock music
around the clock to drive him from his lair? A British angler has
used the music of Eminem for a similar purpose.

Mark Elmer of Birmingham reported that the fish just weren't
biting in Chelmsley Wood until he happened to bring his boom
box along. Contrary to the long-held belief that it is best to be quiet
around fish so as not to startle them away, playing the
Eminem tracks caused the fish to go into a biting frenzy. Mr. Elmer
now says he catches fish by the bucketful from using his sonic
secret weapon.

St. Peter confronts a guy at the Pearly Gates. "Sorry, buddy, but
you told one too many lies while you lived on earth. I can't allow
you to come in here."

"Aw, St. Peter. Can't you remember when you, too, were a
fisherman?"

WHAT DID THE MUMMY
SARDINE SAY TO HER
CHILDREN WHEN THEY SAW
A SUBMARINE?

Waldo agreed to take his little brother Wally fishing while their parents went shopping. When the parents came home, Waldo said, "I'll never take Wally fishing again. I didn't get a single bite."

"I'm sure he'll be quiet next time," said his father. "Just explain to him that noise will scare the fish and they'll swim away."

"It wasn't that," said Waldo. "He ate my bait."

A couple of anglers are boating on a lake at an Indian reservation. All of a sudden, the lake is surrounded by some natives who are more than a bit upset that these guys are fishing on their property. Off in the distance, the fishermen hear the beat of a drum. One of the guys says, "I don't like the sound of those drums."

A moment later, a distant voice yells, "He's not our regular drummer!"

Pelican one: Pretty good fish you have there.

Pelican two: Well, it fills the bill.

Three old geezers were sitting on a bench in New York City's
Central Park. The one in the middle was reading a newspaper while
the other two were pretending to fish. A policeman on the beat
watched them as they baited imaginary hooks, cast their lines and
reeled in their fake catches.

"Do you know these two?" the cop asked the guy reading the
paper.

"Sure. They're buddies of mine."

"Well, they're disturbin' the other people. You better get them
outta here!"

"Yes, officer," said the guy. With that, he furiously began rowing.

Two old fishermen, Carmine and Fenster, were out in some rough
weather when Carmine suddenly lost his dentures over the side
of the boat. Fenster, a sly old codger, decided to play a prank on
Carmine. He removed his own false teeth, tied them on his line
and made believe he had caught the missing dentures. He pulled
the line in, unhooked the dentures and gave them to his friend.
Carmine thanked Fenster and slipped the dentures into his mouth.
After a few moments, he pulled them out and said disgustedly,
"They're not mine. They don't fit!" So he threw them back in the
water.

Fish 'n Fingers

Actor James Caan, appearing on *The Tonight Show*, told host Jay Leno about the time he went fishing with a friend and caught a five-pound bass. "I took the fish home and prepared the hot oil and the bread crumbs and all of that stuff. And when I cut into this fish, my knife hit something hard. It was my thumb."

Fish & CHIPS

After a torrential downpour, California Highway Patrol Officer Alvin Yamaguchi was directing traffic around a flooded intersection in the Los Angeles suburb of Irvine when he pulled a carp over. That's not a misprint. It was a 35-pound carp that had escaped from a nearby reservoir. Yamaguchi asked for the carp's license and registration. When the carp refused a breathalyzer test on the grounds that it might prove fatal, Yamaguchi nabbed it, throwing it to drier ground where they took pictures and prints. Well, okay, maybe not prints- but he needed the pictures, because no one would ever believe him otherwise. Wonder if the fish wound up in the cooler or got off the hook?

Old Fisbin was leaning over the bar, crying in his beer. "My wife says if I ever go fishin' again, she's going to leave me."

"Gee, that's tough," his friend commiserated.

"Yeah," sniffed Fisbin, wiping a tear from his eye. "I'm sure going to miss her."

Mrs. Jones was trying to teach her second graders the importance of patience. She showed the class a picture of a boy fishing and said, "See, even things that are fun, like fishing, require patience. Why, look at that boy. He's sitting very quietly, waiting. He's very patient. Okay boys and girls, if you were going to go fishing, what is the single most important thing to have?"

A voice from the back of the class rang out, "Bait!"

A guy went on an ocean fishing expedition and fell overboard in shark-infested waters. The guy couldn't swim and screamed for help. A lawyer who happened to be on the trip dove in to save him. All of a sudden, sharks formed a two-lane convoy and escorted the lawyer and the guy he was dragging to shore. Safely ashore, the guy thanked the lawyer profusely, but was extremely puzzled. "I don't understand it," he said. "Why did the sharks do that?"

"Simple," replied the lawyer. "Professional courtesy."

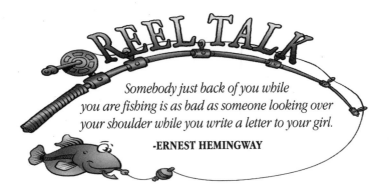

Somebody just back of you while you are fishing is as bad as someone looking over your shoulder while you write a letter to your girl.

-ERNEST HEMINGWAY

A fishing boat goes down with only one man surviving and he's washed ashore on a remote island inhabited by cannibals. They capture him and tie him to a stake, where they proceed to nick him with their spears and drink his blood. This goes on for two weeks. The guy can't take it any longer and asks to see the chief. When the cannibal leader arrives the guy says, "Look, chief...either let me go or kill me. I'm tired of being stuck for the drinks."

Egbert was bragging to all his buddies about the humongous fish he caught.

"How big was it?" asked his friend, Willie.

"It was the biggest I've ever seen."

Willie said, "That doesn't tell me very much. Can you measure it with your hands?"

Egbert looked around the room and responded, "Yeah, but we'll have to go outside."

The wife is telling her friend about her recent vacation to Venice, Italy. The friend asks, "What did your husband like best about it- the art, the statues or the architecture?"

"Oh, none of those things. His favorite was being able to sit in the hotel and fish from the window."

You Never Know What You Might Pull Up

The word "Granny" conjures up images of lace doilies, not lace panties, but that was all Mrs. Beryl Wonson of Gloucester, Massachusetts was left with after a battle with a 755 pound tuna.

People in Gloucester take their fishing seriously, so after the genteel grandmother hooked into the huge fish, there was no going back, not even for her pants. She was buckled into a harness which started slipping down her back, pushing her trousers as it went. Naturally, she wanted to pull them back up, but her hands were busy gripping the pole. Something had to give and she decided to lose her pants rather than the fish. She kicked them free and continued the battle in her lace trimmed bikini bottoms. The men on board were embarrassed, but fishermen and gentlemen all, they averted their eyes and followed the epic battle.

When it was finally over, Mrs. Wonson got her pants back and reported that she had worked up a sweat, but the wind through her legs was very chilly. She'll always remember the incident as the day she almost caught a fish and a cold on the same outing.

WHAT IS HALF FISH AND HALF ZEBRA?

Three guys were fishing by a lake when, suddenly, an angel appeared and said "I'm here to help you heel, not to fish. What may I do for you?"

One of the guys immediately said, "I've had chronic back pain for ages." With that, the angel touched his back and he felt relief at once.

The second guy, who wore extremely thick glasses, told the angel of his horrible eyesight. The angel removed his glasses, tossed them into the lake and presto- the guy had 20/20 vision!

"Don't come near me!" exclaimed the third fisherman. "I'm on disability!"

Twin Fins

Gina and Toni Grimaldi are identical twins, even more alike than most. Fishing on a charter out of Bermuda, Toni hooked a blue marlin and fought it for 38 minutes before bringing it to gaff. Two hours later, her sister Gina hooked into a blue marlin and battled for 38 minutes before landing it. And naturally, the marlins could have been twins as well. They both weighed exactly 187 pounds.

A STRIPED BASS

Barney: Say, Ralph, 'member when we took that fishing trip last summer and your car broke down?

Ralph: Yeah, what a fiasco that was.

Barney: Sure was ... and remember how we wound up spending the night at that farm owned by that good-looking, wealthy widow?

Ralph: Sure do.

Barney: And remember how we slept in the guest wing of her gigantic house while she slept in her wing- and then in the morning we got our car started and headed up to the lake to go fishing?

Ralph: Yep.

Barney: Well, here it is, a year later and I got a letter from her lawyer.

Ralph: Oh, really?

Barney: Ralph, did you by any chance get up in the middle of the night and go visit her?

Ralph: Well, yeah.

Barney: And did you use my name instead of telling her yours?

Ralph: Sorry about that ... I did. Why do you ask?

Barney: Because she just died and left me everything.

One day at the fishing hole, an elephant happened to notice a snapping turtle sunning itself on a rock.

Without provocation, the elephant went over to the snapper, picked it up with his trunk and threw it through the air over the trees. A fisherman with his line in the water nearby, said, "Hey, why'd you do that? That turtle was minding its own business."

"Well," replied the elephant, "I was drinking water and I happened to remember that same snapper took a chunk out of my trunk twenty years ago."

"Man! What a memory!" exclaimed the fisherman.

"All elephants have it," responded the pachyderm modestly. "It's called turtle recall."

HOOK, LINE, & STINKER

Q: What do Texans call sushi?

A: Bait

A businesswoman vacationing in Boca Raton is strolling along the beach when she runs into a fisherman who, with his line in the water, is patiently waiting for a bite. The fisherman likes what he sees and says, "Hey, hon, would you like a little company?"

She replies, "Do you have one to sell?"

"I have good news and bad news about your movie script," said the agent to the author of *Fish Tales*.

"What's the good news?" asked the author.

"Spielberg loved your script...He just ate it up."

"And the bad news?"

"Spielberg's my dog."

Farnsworth, affectionately known as the "fishing fibber" for tales about "the big one that got away", was terribly ill. His wife, visiting him in the hospital, asked the doctor how he was doing.

The doctor responded, "I'm afraid he's lying at death's door."

"Imagine that," said the wife. "He's about to meet his maker and he's still lying."

Playing Chicken-In-The-Sea

The sea off Morro Bay, California teems with all sorts of life, and not all of it defers to fishermen. In 1998, an angler aboard a sport fishing boat hooked a salmon. It looked to be an easy catch, but suddenly, a seal grabbed the fish and wouldn't let go. The fisherman and the seal fought it out for quite some time, neither one giving ground- er, water. The battle see-sawed back and forth. The fisherman was stymied, the seal was stymied and the poor fish was totally screwed.

Finally, the captain ordered the other anglers to pull their lines from the water, and then cranked up the vessel's powerful engines to make a run directly for the seal. Unfortunately, the seal, although protected by federal law, didn't have his attorney with him at the time. He finally relinquished the fish and dove to safety as the multi-ton speeding vessel bore down on him.

It took a million dollars in equipment, violation of the Marine Mammal Protection Act and the efforts of several men, but they finally got their trophy- one badly chewed up fish.

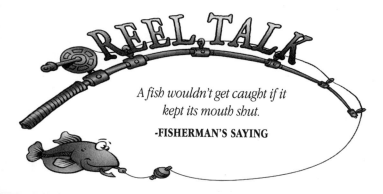

A fish wouldn't get caught if it kept its mouth shut.

-FISHERMAN'S SAYING

A duck walks into a convenience store and asks, "Do you sell any bait here?"

The manager says, "No, we don't carry bait."

The next day the duck walks into the store and asks, "Do you sell any bait?"

The manager says, "No, we don't have bait here."

The third day the duck walks into the store and asks, "Do you have any bait?"

The manager says, "Look! If I told you once, I told you three times-we don't have any bait here! The next time you come in here asking for bait, I'm gonna nail your webbed feet to the wall!"

The next day the duck enters the store and asks, "Do you have any nails?"

The manager says, "No. We don't sell nails here."

The duck says, "Good. Do you have any bait?"

WHAT DO YOU SAY TO A GUY WITH HIS LURE IN THE SEAWEED?

At Sunday school, the teacher was leading a class discussion on what Noah might have done to pass time on the Ark.

"I think he went fishing," said one little girl.

The little boy sitting beside her gave her a look and piped up, "What...with only two worms?!?"

Whale of a Tale

One of the inspirations for author Herman Melville's classic *Moby-Dick* was the true-life sinking of the whaling ship "Essex" by a whale in 1820. Captain George Pollard and several others aboard the ship resorted to cannibalism to survive the long ordeal.

Long after the tragedy, Pollard was approached by a relative of one of the lost crew members, who timidly asked whether the captain remembered him. "Remember him!?" exclaimed Pollard. "Hell, I ate him!"

Then there was the aristocratic fish...His ancestors swam under the QE2.

"YOUR FLY'S DOWN!"

The game warden approached a boy who was fishing by the lake.

"Hey, son. Can't you read? The sign says 'No Fishing Allowed.'"

The boy whispered, "I'm fishing very quietly, sir."

A guy rushes into a fishing supply place and hurriedly says, "I have to catch the ferry and I need some bait, quick!"

The store clerk, with a quizzical look on his face, responds, "I dunno, sir...I don't think we have any bait that a ferry would like."

A fisherman was arrested and brought to court for having caught fourteen more striped bass than the law allowed.

The judge asked, "How do you plead?"

"Guilty, your Honor," was the reply.

"That'll be 75 dollars plus costs," said the judge.

The fisherman paid the fine, then inquired of the judge, "Your Honor, if you don't mind, would it be possible to make some copies of the court record to take home to show my buddies?"

How Not to Catch a Shark

Ah, the Florida Keys. Paradise. The sun, the sand, the surf, the sharks... well, almost paradise.

Richard Burkle was fishing near the Seven Mile Bridge one day in the summer of 1961. The weather was hot and the humidity was so high that Burkle felt wetter than the fish he was going after. Totally drained from the extended battle with the big shark he had just hooked, Burkle decided to end the contest early. He would use his pistol to bring the landing to a swift conclusion.

If you ever hear anyone use the expression "It's as easy as shooting fish in a barrel," pay close attention to the "barrel" part, because otherwise, shooting fish ain't so easy. Burkle was about to pull the trigger when the shark jerked, making him slip on the wet embankment and causing him to shoot himself in the left leg.

Now that there was blood all over, the shark was even more agitated. Burkle decided that it was the better part of valor to crawl away before the creature had him stuffed and mounted.

Bleeding profusely, Burkle managed to crawl through the thick undergrowth to his car and drive himself to a police station. He was then transported on to the hospital where they took out the bullet, but couldn't restore his pride.

At least Burkle will always have the story of the one that got away- him!

The fisherman had a shopping cart full of angling equipment as he made his way to the cash register. Watching the cashier ring up hundreds of dollars worth of gear, he sighed, "You know, if you'd start selling fish here, you could save me a bundle of money."

A girl went fishing for the first time with her boyfriend. As they sat in their rowboat on the lake, she asked, "How much was that red and white thing?"

"Oh, you mean the float? That's only about a nickel."

"I guess I owe you a nickel then. My float just sank."

Who Needs a Crib?

Pro golfer and avid fisherman Mike Hulbert landed a big one- 8 lbs, 3 oz. to be exact. "He's just perfect for mounting," said Hulbert after taking a look at his newborn son.

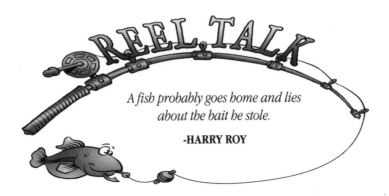

A fish probably goes home and lies about the bait he stole.

-HARRY ROY

Brad Pitt: The Catch Who Caught Himself

Brad Pitt had to learn how to fly-cast for his role in the 1990s flick *A River Runs Through It*. Practice sessions were held on various Hollywood rooftops and were going along quite well- that is, until Pitt hooked himself so firmly in the back of the head that the hook had to be removed with pliers.

A couple of frogs are sitting on a lily pad at the fishing hole. A fly breezes by and one of the frogs snatches it with his tongue. The other frog, looking on, says, "Time sure is fun when you're having flies."

In Miami, a fisherman ran into a dockside bar and said to the bartender, "Quick, give me a drink before the fight starts."

The bartender gave him a drink and he knocked it back and ran out the door. A moment later, he ran back in and said, "Give me a drink before the fight starts."

Once again, he downed the booze and dashed out. A minute later he was back again and said, "I need a drink before the fight starts."

The bartender slammed down the bottle and snapped, "Wait a minute! Who's going to pay for all these drinks?"

The fisherman said, "Uh oh, the fight's about to start."

A banker went fishing with one of his customers. They were out on a boat in the river when the vessel smashed into a rock and tipped over, spilling the guys into the drink. The customer noticed the banker flailing away and said, "Say, can you float alone?"

"Oh, c'mon!" exclaimed the banker. "I'm drowning and you want to talk business!?!"

Riley and Baxter were out on the lake at the crack of dawn. They cast for trout, sat silently and kept still so they wouldn't frighten off the fish. Five hours later, Baxter shifted his feet.

"What is it with you?" snapped Riley. "Make up your mind. Did you come here to fish or to dance?"

Maybe you've heard about the new glass-bottomed boats. Now the fish can boast about how big the guy was they got away from.

WHAT KIND OF MONEY DO FISHERMEN MAKE?

An avid angler on a fishing trip was at it for almost two weeks before he caught his first fish. When he got back to his hotel, he texted his wife: "I've got one. She's a real beauty...weighs seven pounds. I'll be home in a couple of days."

His wife responded with this text: "I've got one as well. She also weighs seven pounds and is a real beauty, too. Come home at once."

A guy goes ice fishing in Minnesota for the first time. He's not having any luck at all, but another guy sitting close by is pulling up fish left and right. The novice ice fisherman asks the guy, "What's the trick?"

The ice fisherman mumbles, "Mmumottameepdammrmsmmrm."

"What'd you say?"

"Mmumottameepdammrmsmmrm."

"I still don't understand you."

With that, the ice fisherman opens his thermos, spits into it a couple of times and then says, "I said you've got to keep the worms warm."

A lonely Bubba signed up for a dating service, explaining that he'd had a lot of trouble finding his significant other. The reason seemed to be his unrealistic expectations. He demanded that the candidate be cute and short, an expert swimmer, love the outdoors and be a fish fanatic. He was thrilled to receive a reply the following week- until he opened it and found a picture of a penguin.

Dam Nuisance

Steve Wagner of Medford, Oregon decided to get in a bit of fishing before going to work. He stopped by the Savage Rapids Dam at the Rogue River, parked his SUV and went to see how they were biting. He looked back a few seconds later to see his SUV rolling downhill. He ran in front of it, but was unable to slow it against the steep grade. He tried jumping into the moving vehicle, but only managed to get in halfway and couldn't apply the brake. Steve bailed out and ran downhill, yelling warnings to the people below. The SUV bounced off a tree and crashed into the river, taking Steve's cell phone, wallet, digital camera and fishing tackle along with it.

The truck was later recovered, but not Steve's pride. "I'll be in the book of dummies for eternity. My wife is definitely going to rescind my fishing privileges."

The answer is: Bassinet

The question: What makes fishermen happy?

A guy saw a fisherman catch a giant trout, only to throw it back into the water. A few minutes later, he nabbed another huge trout but tossed that away, too. Then he caught a little trout, smiled and put it into his cooler for safekeeping. The guy who was watching the fisherman asked, "How come you threw away the big fish and kept the small one?"

The fisherman replied, "Small frying pan."

A couple of Eskimos went fishing on an extremely frigid day. They lit a fire in the bottom of their kayak to warm up, but moments later the blaze raged out of control and their boat sank.

The moral of the story: You can't have your kayak and heat it, too.

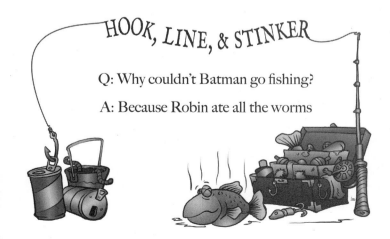

HOOK, LINE, & STINKER

Q: Why couldn't Batman go fishing?

A: Because Robin ate all the worms

Whole Lotta Shark Shakin'

If you're ever face to face with a great white shark, remember to whip out your MP3 player and play some AC/DC for it- although it might be a little tricky getting those headphones on.

Scientists have discovered that the fish fancy the music of AC/DC, specifically *You Shook Me All Night Long*. In fact, it calms them down, making them more inquisitive and less aggressive. Researchers say the tune has even been known to make the huge sharks nuzzle.

A safety note for divers planning an underwater rock concert with just any old hard rock: You may attract a whole bunch of head-banging sharks, so be careful not to wind up in the "Nosh Pit".

Fishing in the Keys

Out on the soft green banks of the Cedar River near Osage, Iowa, a man was fishing one day and hooked a big catfish. The battle went on for quite a while, but the catfish finally outsmarted him and swam away.

When the man returned to his car, he found that his keys were missing. He guessed that they had fallen out of his pocket during the epic struggle between man and fish.

The following week, he was back at the same spot and this time managed to land a fair-sized catfish. Later, while cleaning it at home, he got his car keys back- he caught the very fish that swallowed them!

A guy is eating a bald eagle and gets caught by the game warden. He's brought to trial for killing an endangered species. The judge says, "Are you aware that eating a bald eagle is a federal offense?"

The guy answers, "Yes, but I have an explanation... I got lost in the woods and didn't have anything to eat for two weeks. I saw this bald eagle swooping down for fish in the lake. I figured I might be able to steal some fish as the eagle grabbed them. Unfortunately, when I went to grab for the fish, my fist hit the eagle in the head and killed 'im. I reckoned that, since the eagle was dead, I might as well eat it since it would be a waste to just let it rot."

After a brief recess, the judge comes back with his ruling. "Due to the extreme conditions you endured, added to the fact that the bald eagle's death was accidental rather than intentional, I find you not guilty." As an aside, the judge asks the guy, "By the way, what does a bald eagle taste like?"

The guy responds, "The best way to describe it is that it tastes like a cross between an owl and an egret."

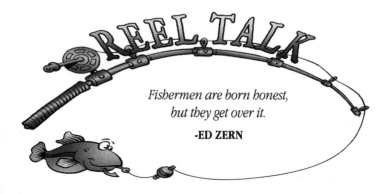

Fishermen are born honest,
but they get over it.

-ED ZERN

A wheeler-dealer entrepreneur was on vacation at the beach when he noticed what appeared to be a lazy fisherman sitting leisurely by the water with his pole propped up in the sand and his line cast out.

"Hey, bud," said the entrepreneur. "You're not going to catch any fish that way. You should be at work, anyway."

The fisherman responded, "Oh yeah? Why should I be at work?"

"Because you'll make money and then you can buy a boat which will enable you to catch more fish," said the entrepreneur.

"Why do you think that would be good for me?" questioned the fisherman.

The entrepreneur was becoming a bit irritated answering the fisherman's questions. "That would be good for you because you'd eventually be able to buy a bigger boat and hire other fishermen to work for you," he said.

"Why is that so good for me?" asked the fisherman.

WHAT DO YOU GET IF YOU CROSS A WHALE WITH A COMPUTER?

Now the entrepreneur was highly agitated. "Look...you don't seem to get the point. When all is said and done, you could wind up with a whole fleet of fishing boats and amass great fortunes."

"And then what would happen?" asked the fisherman.

The entrepreneur, steaming mad, barked, "What would happen?!? You'd become filthy rich and would never have to work again! You could spend the rest of your years sitting on this beach fishing without a care in the world."

The fisherman smiled at the entrepreneur and said, "And what do you think I'm doing right now?"

Pete takes the grieving widow of his old fishing buddy out in his bass boat to show her just where the fatal accident occurred the day before. After circling the spot for twenty minutes he looks up and says, "I know this is around the place where Al stood up and fell in. I'm sure this is where I radioed the ranger and he brought the police, but for the life of me, I can't find it."

"Find what?" sniffled Al's widow.

"The chalk outline."

A FOUR TON KNOW IT ALL

Gus and Mus, two old fishing buddies, were comparing their exploits, each trying to out do the other.

"Once, up in Newfoundland during a full North Atlantic gale, I caught a herring," Gus said. "And I'm tellin' you, Mus, it was the biggest herring that ever lived. It weighed at least 500 pounds!"

"That's nothing, Gus," retaliated Mus. "Down in the Keys, I pulled up my line and on the hook was a ship's lamp. On the bottom, there was the date 1392...a full century before Columbus! And get this... inside the lamp, the light was still burning!"

Gus studied his buddy's face for a few moments before cracking a smile. "Tell you what, Mus...let's compromise. I'll knock 475 pounds off the herring and you blow out the light!"

Sherlock Holmes and Dr. Watson were on a fishing trip deep in the English countryside. They had retired for the evening and were lying there, looking up at the sky. Holmes said, "Watson, look up. What do you see?"

"Well, I see thousands of stars."

"And what does that mean to you?"

"Well, I guess it means we will have another fine day for fishing tomorrow. What does it mean to you, Mr. Holmes?"

"To me, my dear Watson, it means someone has stolen our tent."

Sweet Success

Bennie Parker of Mount Pleasant, Michigan was enjoying a pleasant day of fishing with his party when he ran out of bait. Going to get more was impractical, but he found an alternative when he saw one of the kids eating Gummi worms- that popular, multi-colored squishy candy.

"Hey, it's worth a shot," Bennie thought. He put one on his hook and soon enough caught a fish. More Gummi worms went into the drink and out came more fish. Now Parker always brings a goodly supply along to use when the fish simply aren't biting anything else.

Little Johnny is out fishing with his grandfather. They're sitting by the river, waiting and waiting for the fish to bite. Finally, to break up the boredom, little Johnny's grandfather decides to teach his grandson a lesson. He takes out a flask of whiskey from his hip pocket and pours it into a glass. Then he reaches for the bait, pulls out a couple of worms and puts them in the glass full of liquor. The worms become lifeless almost immediately. "Look here, Johnny," his grandfather says. "See that? Those worms have died. What does that tell you, son?"

"Simple, Grandpa," little Johnny answers. "Drink whiskey and you won't get worms."

That Sinking Feeling

Captain Paul Campbell, of the 38 foot fishing boat Little David out of Martha's Vineyard, was trolling near Block Island when he hooked a whopper. His boat stopped its forward motion and began being towed backwards, its transom crashing squarely into the swell and throwing up huge amounts of spray. The boat shuddered and shook while the propellers spun futilely at full speed ahead. Campbell figured it had to be a whale of some sort, but it was even worse than that. Soon his stern was nearly awash and he was forced to cut loose his fishing line to save the boat.

It turned out to be a good call, for a few moments later his "catch" surfaced just astern- a US Navy submarine.

The answer is Three Men and a Baby.

And the question? What do you get when four men go fishing and one comes back without having a single catch?

Here's a guy standing in cold water up to his liver throwing the world's most expensive clothesline at trees.

-P.J. O'ROURKE,
on fly fishing

Love Bite

They say all the nuts roll downhill to Florida, and in this case it
might be true. A scuba diver made a habit out of kissing nurse
sharks, but one fateful day, one of the normally docile creatures
took umbrage to the diver's unwanted advances. Since sharks
lack arms and hands with which to slap molesting humans, they
bite them in the face instead. That's exactly what happened in
this particular incident, with the interspecies smooch resulting in
the world's worst case of lip lock. When the shark finally let go, a
swarm of snappers came in to give the hapless diver pecks on what
was left of his lips.

Fortunately, there was an expert plastic surgeon at the nearby
hospital who managed to reassemble most of the man's face in a
long and complicated operation.

The diver's takeaway from all this? He now says that he'll never kiss
another nurse shark- while it is upside down.

Maybe you've heard the one about the fisherman who caught a 220
pound tuna, but had to throw it back. It was a piano tuner.

Q: Why does a fish take things in his mouth?
A: Because he doesn't have any hands.

Loony Laws of the Land- And Sea
Laughable legislation that just
might still be on the books!

Talk About Fishing Yarns!

New Jersey, both a popular fisherman's destination and ground
zero for loony laws, has this one on the books: It is illegal for a man
to knit during fishing season. If you get caught by the local game
warden, you might try claiming that your knitting needles are really
tiny harpoons for crappies.

You're Going To Need A Bigger Jon Boat

If you like going after the really big ones, you might as well stay out
of Nebraska. The government killjoys there have gone so far as to
outlaw fishing for whales. Because of this shortsightedness,
Nebraska stands a very real chance of a whale population explosion.

Sloshed To The Gills

Oklahoma has a strict prohibition against getting fish drunk.
Presumably, the game wardens there carry little tiny breathylizers.

**WHAT KIND OF FISH DO YOU
FIND IN A BIRD CAGE?**

How's A Girl Expected To Hook Her Prize Catch?

In Montana, it is illegal for married women to go fishing alone on Sunday. But before you feel too sorry for them, it is illegal for unmarried women to go fishing alone at all! Maybe women in Montana need to go over to Idaho and fish for some new lawmakers. Of course in Idaho, it is unlawful to fish for trout from the back of a giraffe so maybe the gals should try their luck in Wyoming instead.

Second Guessing The Second City

In Chicago, it is illegal to fish in your pajamas. You may wonder what originally inspired this law but remember, Playboy's Hef has been angling in his pajamas for years- just not for fish.

No Fish Fingers Please

If Indiana anglers catch fish with their bare hands the long arm of the law will reach out and catch them. Pennsylvania has a similar rule stating that the only part you can catch a fish by is its mouth. Those who like to fish with their hands will best stay out of those states where they'll either be nipped or nabbed.

Twirling Vs. Trolling

In Tennessee, there's a law against catching fish with a lasso. If the fish happens to get tangled in your line does that count? And really, to be fair, if someone is good enough to actually catch a fish with a lasso, they ought to be allowed to keep it.

A PERCH

A gorilla perched on a tree limb right next to a lake notices that just below him, a lion has cast a line and appears to have settled in for an afternoon of fishing. The gorilla decides to pull a little surprise on the king of the jungle. He leaps from the tree, lands on the lion's back and lets out a ferocious growl. He catches the lion by surprise, alright. The lion lets go of the pole and runs out from underneath the gorilla's grasp straight into the water.

Now the gorilla knows the lion is going to be enraged, so he takes off and runs into the woods. Once the lion regains his senses and realizes what's happened, he becomes hopping mad and begins to take chase.

The gorilla figures he's no match for the lion's speed, so he looks for a place to duck for cover. He spots a tent and runs inside, where he sees a hunter sitting there, reading the newspaper. When the hunter notices the gorilla, he immediately bolts from the tent. The gorilla quickly takes the hunter's hat from the chair, puts it on, sits down, grabs the newspaper and covers his face as if to be reading it.

Meanwhile, the lion, in hot pursuit, comes to a screeching halt when he reaches the tent. He peers inside and sees someone reading the newspaper. "Hey, buddy," roars the lion, "Did you see anyone come running by here?"

The gorilla never looks up from behind the paper and says, "You mean the gorilla that jumped you from behind?"

The lion groans, "Oh, no. You mean to tell me it's in the paper already?"

Two Chicago tourists, heading to Florida for vacation, had been tooling down hot, dry and dusty roads for hours when they happened to spot a tranquil little spring-fed pond. Sitting on the bank, a small barefoot boy was fishing.

"Yo, Kid!" called one of the tourists. "Are there any snakes in this pond?"

"No, sir," said the lad.

With that, the two dusty and overheated men stripped down to their undies and dove into the water.

After frolicking for a few minutes, one of the men surfaced near the boy and said, "Say, Son, I was just wondering. How do you know for sure there aren't any snakes in this water?"

"Easy," the boy smiled. "The gators ate 'em all."

HOOK, LINE, & STINKER

Q: What do fish get if they don't like the bait that fishermen are using?

A: A re-bait

The President and His Pole

"When I was a small boy growing up in Kansas, a friend of mine
and I went fishing, and as we sat there in the warmth of a summer
afternoon on a riverbank we talked about what we wanted to do
when we grew up. I told him that I wanted to be a real major-league
baseball player, a genuine professional like Honus Wagner. My
friend said that he'd like to be President of the United States.
Neither of us got our wish." -*President Dwight D. Eisenhower*

•

Calvin Coolidge, an avid if not successful angler, was once asked
how many trout there were in his favorite fishing spot. The former
president said that estimates ranged up to 45,000 fish. "I haven't
caught them all yet," he added, "but I've intimidated them."

•

"All presidents go fishing, even if they have never fished
before, because the American people and media have respect for
privacy only on two occasions. One of them is prayer, and the other
is fishing, and presidents can't pray all the time." -*Herbert Hoover*

"There were lots of people who committed crimes during the year
(1930) who would not have done so if they had been fishing, and
I assure you that the increase in crime is due to a lack of those
qualities of mind and character which impregnate the soul of every
fisherman except those who get no bites." -*Herbert Hoover*

'Lord, suffer me to catch a fish so large that even I in talking
of it afterward shall have no need to lie.'
-Suggested motto for President Hoover's Fishing Lodge

"I was president and I was fishing on the Snake River in Wyoming, and I had the secret service with me and the military aids and also the White House physician Dr. Bill Lukasz and I hung a big fish - it was a really nice fish - and I snatched the hook and the hook came loose and embedded itself in my face and there I was with this fluffy thing sticking out - you know what a fly looks like - and it wouldn't come out and I didn't know what to do. Finally, Dr. Lukasz put me on the ground and put his foot on my chest and ran a fly line through the hook and held onto it and snatched it out. So that was the biggest one I ever caught." *-Jimmy Carter*

•

"The days a man spends fishing or spends hunting should not be deducted from the time that he's on earth. In other words, if I fish today, that should be added to the amount of time I get to live."
-George H.W. Bush

Q: What do fish use to get in touch with each other?
A: Shell phones

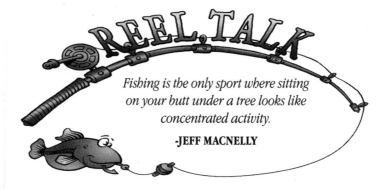

Fishing is the only sport where sitting on your butt under a tree looks like concentrated activity.

-JEFF MACNELLY

Way down south among the magnolia trees and drooping Spanish moss, there was a muddy old fishing hole that seemed almost as if Huck Finn should be lolling back on the grassy banks, passing the sultry summer afternoons dangling a bent pin in the water and spinning yarns.

Little Johnny and his dog Rex were regular visitors to this idyllic spot, and one day while Johnny was fishing, Rex made a wild leap for a bird and landed in the dark, murky water. Finding it cool and refreshing, Rex was not anxious to come out. When he eventually did, he carried the powerful stench of pond scum and bottom mud.

Little Johnny took his reeking Rex home and tied him to a tree far away from the house so he could go to the store for something to clean the smell off of him.

At the store, Johnny picked up the biggest box of industrial strength laundry detergent that he could find and headed to the checkout.

The shopkeeper, kindly old Mr. Withers, asked little Johnny what the detergent was for, and Johnny told him the story about Rex and the dog's need for a good lathering.

WHAT DO YOU GIVE A SEASICK ELEPHANT?

Mr. Withers looked concerned and said, "Johnny, that's some pretty potent stuff there. I don't think it would be good to wash your dog with that."

Little Johnny thought for a moment and decided to take the box anyway.

A week or so later, Johnny was back at the store and Mr. Withers asked him how it went with Rex. "Not so good," Johnny replied. "Rex died."

"Oh, I'm so sorry Johnny," said Mr. Withers. "I did warn you not to use that detergent on him."

"Oh, it wasn't the soap," said little Johnny.

"What did he die of, then?" asked Mr. Withers.

"Well," little Johnny drawled, "The vet thinks it may have been the spin cycle."

Bathroom Graffiti:
Mrs. Paul's Fish Sticks. Does Yours?

The Hookie Hook

There's an old joke about a priest playing golf on Sunday instead of being at church. St. Peter, looking down from heaven, asks God just how he's going to punish him. God says, "You'll see." The priest tees off and hits a 350-yard hole-in-one! St. Peter says to God, "You call that punishment?" God answers, "Aha, but who's he going tell?"

In a reel life story, nine-year-old Jarrett Hillman could relate to that. Jarrett and his dad left Beach Haven, New Jersey's Tuna Marlin Club on the morning of June 15, 2011 for some fishing out on the Atlantic Ocean. Some five miles out and 9 hours later, Jarrett felt a tug on his pole. This wasn't your ordinary tug. This was a capital "T"- as in thresher- tug. Jarrett had hooked a thresher shark. A big one. A lot bigger than Jarrett himself. Yet, in a 45-minute tug of war, the 72-pound youngster was able to pull in the 248.5 lb. monster (which measured 75 inches from the nose to the fork in the tail and 70 inches from the tip of the tail to the fork). In the process, Jarrett established an International Game Fishing Association record in the age 10 and under "small fry" division.

But "aha", as God said in the golf groaner, who was Jarrett going to tell? While he was setting a world-class mark, his third grade classmates were sitting in school.

"One brisk morning spent fishing on a misty lake can bring home to a child the beauty, drama and fragility of our natural heritage in a way a thousand classroom presentations never could."
-President George H.W. Bush, in a 1989 message
on the observance of National Fishing Week

BUMPER SNICKERS

FISHERMEN GET THE BLUES

• • •

WOMEN WANT ME, FISH FEAR ME

• • •

WHEN FISHERMEN DRINK,
THEY ASSIGN A DESIGNATED DIVER

• • •

FISH STORIES TOLD HERE

• • •

GET REEL!

• • •

I FISH, THEREFORE I LIE

• • •

I CATCH FISH BY THE TALE

• • •

OLD FISHERMEN NEVER DIE,
THEY JUST LOSE THEIR MUSSELS

Fisherman's Prayer

God grant that I may live
to fish until my dying day,
and when the final cast is made
and life has slipped away,
I pray that God's great landing net
will catch me in its sweep,
and in His mercy, God will judge me
big enough to keep.